Taking

Authority

Over

Your

Neighborhood

Written by P. Lee May

Illustrated by Juan Bran and P. Lee May

Unless otherwise indicated scripture quotations are taken from **The King James Bible** (KJV).

Scripture quotations marked (AMP) are taken from **The Amplified Bible**.

Scripture quotations marked (MSG) or MSG come from **The Message Bible**.

ISBN-13: 978-0-9846410-5-5
ISBN-10: 0-9846410-5-X

Taking Authority Over Your Neighborhood
God's Heartbeat LLC
P. R. Lee
9624 South Cicero #414
Oak Lawn, IL 60453
Email: admin@godsheartbeat-inc.com
Email: godsheartbeat_inc@yahoo.com

Dedication

This book is dedicated to Father God, Holy Spirit, and the Lord Jesus Christ. I also dedicate it to: Dolores A. Lee (my Mama), Evangelist Marilynn James, Rev. Anne Johnson, Barb Ost, Yolanda Thomas, and Sister Irene Davis.

These women encouraged me to write the book with their prayers and experiences. God used them individually and mightily in my life.

Table of Contents

Introduction

I'm trying to remember when did it first hit me that I could stand on the word myself? I'm trying to think when I decided that God is not a respecter of persons? I'm trying to remember when I first agreed with the word of God? Honestly, I can't remember when I received the first revelation.

All I know is: I can share with you the results. I can share how to protect your family from danger. I can share how to stop a family member from being tormented with additional debts they do not deserve from a dead relative. I can share how to change your neighborhood because I believe that when I live in a neighborhood, I rule. I have authority because I belong to God.

You see I read how God protected the children of Israel from pests while they were in Egypt and the Egyptians were plagued with flies and frogs. I read how God used David to defeat a huge giant and his gang that was terrorizing David's people.

I read how God allowed the children of Israel to borrow expensive things from their masters then He cancelled their debts completely. I read how ***every time the children of Israel entered into a new neighborhood: <u>they took over</u>***.

So if it happened for Joshua and the

children of Israel, it can happen for me. If angels could push down the walls of Jericho, then they can protect my neighbors, my family, and me from danger. I decided to believe God. I decided to work the word of God.

Since God is not a respecter of persons then what He did for my neighborhood, my family, my friends, and me; He can do for you!

After reading this book, you will understand that you don't have to have the drug dealer selling drugs, gang members marking up your property, and thieves breaking into your neighbor's house and/or your house because you live in the neighborhood. **You have the authority to change your neighborhood**.

Chapter One:
Getting Rid of Pests

We, my husband, our three daughters, and I, finally moved out of the basement of his family's building into this house on 69th and Dorchester in Chicago. We purchased it from an older woman who wanted to sell it because the house was too much for her.

I got married because I was in love and pregnant. The family building we lived in had a fire when our twins were six months old and their three-year-old cousin died from smoke inhalation. Since we could no longer live in the basement of the building until it was repaired by the insurance company, we lived with my sister in her apartment temporarily.

My husband wanted to be near his mother (she lived on the second floor of that building), so we moved back into the basement once it was completely repaired. (We still didn't have separate rooms only dedicated areas with furniture for the living room, our beds, and the kitchen. The only doors were the bathroom and entrance doors.)

When we moved back, my husband promised we would move out eventually into our own place. It was not until after our third daughter was born that he agreed to move. When she was two years old and right before the twins made four, I received Jesus Christ into my heart.

When we found that place on 69th and Dorchester, I knew it was time to move. The season had changed for us living in the basement of that family building because rats manifested one by one. They had started tunneling their way into that basement apartment through the wood slants in the concrete. I was terrified.

You could hear a rat clawing or chewing. Whenever I heard it, I screamed. My screams echoed all the way up to the third level, which was the second floor. The thing would stop for a moment then start gnawing again. Once it surfaced, my children and I stayed in one spot of the apartment until my husband either killed it or caught it in a trap. Since my husband at that time worked the second and sometimes the third shift, this meant that many nights he was not at home.

My mother-in-law would hear my screams and either call downstairs to see what was going on or would come downstairs herself. If she appeared she would set the trap to catch the rat. Or she may send down my brother-in-law who lived on the first floor. Either way, this thing that was gnawing to get inside our basement apartment where I lived terrified me.

I was grateful when we finally moved in 1981. We moved into this house that was supposed to be a piece of cake to pay for. It was less than what I earned in a month wages and I made a third of my husband's income. We purchased it from that older woman.

She seemed like a nice woman until I had to clean the house after she left. Everything looked okay. I found out quickly that looks can be deceiving. The stove smelled very funny whenever I turned it on. So I proceeded to clean it. I removed the top and discovered to my amazement mice droppings all under the top and throughout the broiler area. I was ready to vomit.

Then I saw a mouse. Remember my husband worked those second and third shifts so I had one of my brothers come by and set traps for mice. After he caught a few, I thought surely all the mice are gone. I was wrong!

My brother, knowing who he was dealing with, spent the night one night after being summoned to my residence while my husband was at work. In the morning, my brother told me I had approximately 40-50 mice or rats on the property. I had small children. This would not work. I had never lived with mice or rats before on a constant basis and did not intend to start now. I had to do something.

My brother set traps and put down poison. I refused to move back into the family building where my mother-in-law lived on the second floor. Besides it had taken me over four years to finally get my ex-husband off of 69th and Aberdeen and out of the basement. We could not go backwards.

I asked God what to do. One morning as my routine was then, I listened for 15 minutes to Marilyn Hickey on the radio. She shared about the pests (they were either locusts or worms) on the trees outside of her house. Marilyn Hickey talked about how she took authority over those things and cursed them off her trees.

The result was those things died and fell off of her trees. The same pests had invaded her neighbors' properties as well. However, she was the only one with no pests on her property for miles after she took authority.

With that testimony still in my ears, I took out the garbage that morning before going to work. Watching a huge gray rat run down the alley toward the 12-flat building next door to us, I realized what I had just heard. Knowing that God is not a respecter of persons, I received revelation for what to do about the pests in my house.

I went inside my house and took authority. I stood in the middle of my living room and cursed mice and rats off of my property. I took authority in Jesus' name from the front of the property to the alley and told all rats and mice that they were no longer welcome on this property. They had to leave!

And they did! Within a week, there was no evidence of mice or rats being on my property all the way to the alley. And when I say gone, they were either dead and removed through traps or totally migrated off the property. Furthermore, I saw rats going toward the properties surrounding us but not on our property. God is good!

Principle #1

God is not a respecter of persons (Acts 10:34 and Romans 2:11). What was available to Marilyn Hickey, a Christian Bible teacher and inside the Bible is available to you and me.

Principle #2

You must recognize **you** have authority. Genesis 1:28 (KJV) says:

> *And God blessed them, and God said unto them, Be fruitful, and multiply, and replenish the earth, and subdue it: and have dominion*

over the fish of the sea, and over the fowl of the air, and over every living thing that moveth upon the earth.

God gave us (you and me) authority in the beginning. We must recognize we have it and operate in it. I had to recognize that I have authority "...*over every living thing that moveth upon the earth.*" This means rats and mice. They move upon the earth.

Once I recognized this principle in my life, I use it everywhere I go. This means when we moved and there were roaches or mice, I cursed them out of my apartment. So when we lived on 77th and Essex, Chicago, IL, and the exterminator came often for roaches for the apartment above but once for us. Those things were evicted by me. They were not allowed to come across our boundaries. Amen.

When I moved into my own home in Maywood, IL, in the spring time the ants tried to invade. They had the wrong person. I put down traps once, told the ants they were not welcomed on my property, and cursed them off my property.

They left. We had no more ants as long as I lived there. Moreover <u>I have never lived with roaches</u> since I discovered this principle.

12

Principle #3

<u>God teaches us how to operate the way He designed us to operate</u>. We have our example of how to operate in faith in Genesis 1(KJV). Starting in verse 3:A, it says "*And God said...*" In verse five it says, "*And God called ...*" Verse six says, "*And God said...*" And verse 10 says:

> *And God called the dry land Earth; and the gathering together of the waters called he Seas: and God saw that it was good.*

Today we still call the Earth "Earth" and the water "seas." It is established forever. Adam, the first man had pure faith in the beginning. He followed God's example. Genesis 2:19 (KJV) says:

> *And out of the ground the Lord God formed every beast of the field, and every fowl of the air; and brought them unto Adam to see what he would call them: and whatsoever Adam called every living creature, that was the name thereof.*

So whatever assignment God gave him to do, Adam had the faith to complete the work. He operated just like God because Adam saw it in his mind then called it. Every animal named by Adam still has their same original name today. So the way we are supposed to operate is to call things in existence.

We have gotten away from operating the way God intended. Thus, God teaches us how to use our faith His way. He longs and desires for us to operate the way He originally designed us, which is just like Adam did. Depending on the situation and circumstances, God builds our faith in small doses. Zechariah 4:10a says:

> For who hath despised the day of small things?

Principle #4

Faith building starts at home: inside your own home. If you are to rule and take authority over anything, any territory, any community, state, country, nation, or neighborhood, you begin ruling in your own home first.

I learned how to build my faith at home for greater victories and accomplishments. It started in my house with conquering those pests: roaches, ants, and rodents. It continued into different circumstances like my job, neighborhood, schools, city, state, country, and for other people. If God can do it for me, He can do it for you too.

Chapter 2:
Protecting My Property

Since I discovered I had authority over things inside my home because of Jesus, I exercised my authority outside of my home. Remember that house I purchased in Maywood, IL? There were two major situations that happened that I exercised my authority over.

The first one was when I walked to the garage one day and I discovered that some local gang member decided to express him/herself by writing in silver on my yellow wooden fence. It was done with silver paint so that it would not be immediately noticeable and would illuminate at night.

This would not do! When I returned home that evening, I got the yellow paint I had in the garage and painted over the silver markings. The gang member did not get the message that their graffiti was not welcome on my property because it happened a second time. The second time it happened, it was time for me to go into warfare.

Who did the devil think he was; using someone to mark up my property? God gave the property to me and I don't like graffiti. Nor was I going to worry about or care about what the gangs thought.

I got into prayer. **I took authority in the spirit realm**. I told the devil that this is my property and he didn't have any right to mark it up. I released warring angels and ministering angels to protect and surround my property. I asked that any one attempting to write on my property would not be able to. As a matter of fact, that person would feel uncomfortable even coming on my property.

From that time forward after I prayed and took authority, there were no further silver markings on my yellow wooden fence until it was time for me to sell the house. When it appeared that third time, I painted over the silver paint with yellow paint and reminded the enemy I had not left yet. It stopped that third time and did not return as long as I lived on the property.

My daughter visited a neighbor in that area about two years after we left. She said that there were graffiti markings on the door of the garage and on the yellow fence. I know it was me taking my God given authority over the situation that kept the gangs from marking up my property while it was mine.

The second situation occurred when God warned me that the enemy was planning on breaking into my home. When you have a relationship with God, He warns you of impending danger.

We were the prime targets because I was a divorced single female with two adult daughters that were seldom at home. We were always going somewhere or doing something. There were no males in the home or staying on the property as none of us were married. And no man slept overnight. A break-in by burglars was not a situation I desired to happen.

I asked God for wisdom on what to do. And He answered me. I talked it over with my daughters and shared with them what God had given me. We agreed on the time and day to take action.

When the day came, we all walked out of our home to the property line at the edge of the garage. Then the three of us walked around the entire property praying. I prayed the words and they agreed with me by praying in tongues in the spirit.

That day we took authority over our property. I released warring and ministering angels to protect the property from hurt, harm, and danger. I asked God that if anyone attempted to approach our property to burglarize it that they would see our angels and leave. I also asked God that the person would be so uncomfortable that he or she could not break into our property.

I asked God that the moment anyone walking by who thought of breaking into our property; that the police would drive by and drive them off our property.

When we finished we were on the edge of our property line in our north neighbor's driveway up to his locked gate. We had completely surrounded physically as much as possible our property in spiritual prayer. That night we all slept in peace with no fear.

About a month later, a salesman came and introduced me to a home security system. They installed it for free as they were new competition in our neighborhood. I paid a monthly bill directly out of my banking account which kept my bill current. The waived installation costs were $2,000. That was God! So now we had spiritual and natural coverage. God is good!

I learned later that my neighbor across the street kept a gun handy because someone had stolen one of their cars off their parking area behind their home (They don't have a garage). He also personally escorted his wife to her car at night when she was on her way to work to make sure there were no surprises to her.

No one had broken into their home (because someone was always there). I thank God that our home was never broken into and none of our three cars were ever stolen.

One day I was home working inside my house in the front on the second floor. When I went to the back of the first floor to take out the garbage in the afternoon, my north neighbor approached and questioned me about how long I had been home and if I had heard anything?

He quickly explained that someone had broken into his garage and stolen his lawn mower in broad daylight while he was away gambling. He was upset with me as it appeared that the burglar entered his garage through my back yard. In the corner of my backyard was a fenced-in dog house from the previous owner.

We didn't have a dog. So I never went back there nor did we pray over that portion of the property as I couldn't image a reason for anyone entering there if there was no activity there. Nor could I reach it through his driveway when we prayed as he kept his gate locked so when we protected our property we went as far up in his driveway as we could to the second secured gate.

I did not know that there was a working gate between the two properties that went through the doghouse area. It was a gate used by him and the husband of the widow I purchased the home from. My north neighbor knew about it and apparently used it when I was not at home.

The burglar could have been any one in the neighborhood as most of our neighbors knew his gambling schedule. (He liked to have everyone know how much he won gambling and how often he went.) It also had to be someone who knew about the gate as it was obscurely hidden.

This was a secret my north neighbor prided himself as keeping from me that back fired on him. Had I known about it that area that I did not desire going into; it would have been protected in prayer also.

After that I prayed for my north neighbor and my neighbors across the street and that area at the back of my property. The burglaries on their properties stopped. As I continued to pray for them, I began to pray for my other neighbors from all four directions extending out from my house.

Determined to make a difference in Maywood, IL through prayer, I prayed for the properties from Interstate 290 to Madison Street and from 17th Avenue to 9th Avenue. I know from the power of prayer that my neighbors experienced peace from those moments on. As a matter of fact, we began to hear of burglaries north of Madison, east of 9th Avenue, and west of 17th Avenue but not in the area I targeted in prayer. And that continued as long as I was in that neighborhood.

I realized later that I had the faith to exercise in that area as the result of protecting my homes and apartments in Chicago. In that first home on 69th and Dorchester, when we couldn't afford the gas bill and it became too cold to live there in the winter time, the children and I moved out. (My husband had already left and we were waiting there for him to return.)

We stayed with relatives and before we could move back into that house someone had broken in and stole some of our furniture and my grandmother's furs. When it was warmer, I moved in with my children again.

Someone came to the back door while we were there eating dinner and attempted to break in again. It was that night I took authority over the property in prayer and bound anyone from breaking into it again. From that point on and until we finally evacuated the property, no one broke into that house.

I moved closer to my mother in the Avalon Park neighborhood right next to the viaduct and train tracks on 82nd street in Chicago, IL. This helped me as Mom watched my children when I was at work. She walked three blocks to get to my place from her house and this gave her daily exercise.

The apartment building was huge and someone broke in while we were out one day. They took our valued 25" floor model television. While I knew it was the neighbor on the third floor, I couldn't prove it.

Somehow I thought that since we were in an apartment building on the second floor, we were safe. I found out that I had to pray for that apartment to prevent anyone from breaking into it. I realized that **if God didn't protect us no one could**! From that point on, anywhere I moved, I prayed for the property to prevent burglaries, fires, and theft.

Principle #5

Our past experiences and victories build our faith for our major battles. I realize now that my *faith of taking authority* was built from my small victories. David exercised this principle when he faced Goliath. When David brought his brothers food and requested news of how the battle was going for his father; the children of Israel were shaking in their sandals because of Goliath.

David, who had been left alone many times with his father's sheep, could not believe what he was hearing. Why were the Children of Israel allowing this uncircumcised Philistine to torment them? Were they looking at his size? Didn't they know that God was bigger? Didn't they know that God is bigger than any fear?

Had these people even been reading their scrolls or bible? Did they remember their Sabbath or Sunday school lessons? "… *If God be for them who can be against them* (us) … (Romans 8:31b)? Scriptures 1 Samuel 17:32 through 37 say:

> *And David said to Saul, Let no man's heart fail because of him; thy servant will go and fight with this Philistine. 33. And Saul said to David, Thou are not able to go against this Philistine to fight with him: for thou are but a youth and he a man of war from his youth. 34. And David said unto Saul, Thy servant kept his father's sheep, and there came a lion, and a bear, and took a lamb out of the flock. 35. And I went out after him, and smote him, and delivered it out of his mouth: and when he arose*

23

against me, I caught him by his beard, and smote him, and slew him. 36. Thy servant slew both the lion and the bear, and this uncircumcised Philistine shall be as one of them, seeing he hath defied the armies of the living God. 37. David said moreover, The Lord that delivered me out of the paw of the lion, and out of the paw of the bear, he will deliver me out of the hand of this Philistine. And Saul said unto David, Go, and the Lord be with thee.

After David told Saul he would fight Goliath, Saul challenged David's offer. Saul looked at David's size, age, and war experience. None of those things mattered to David. What mattered most was: his experience, victories, and relationship with God.

David had been entrusted with his father's sheep without other attendants. It was during these quiet times alone that David gained victories in God. Once David won over the lion, the size of the bear didn't matter to him. Just like the size of Goliath didn't matter. **But the size of God did matter**!

It is highly possible that because no one knew <u>what God had done for David</u> (his brothers didn't even know), no one knew the faith level David possessed to take authority and protect what was in his charge.

I realized that this is what happened to me. The small victories of keeping burglars from breaking into my homes or apartments helped me to prevent burglars from breaking into my corner lot home in Maywood, IL.

Principle #6

Operating in faith and taking authority extends outside our homes. I started taking authority inside my house and next, I learned to take authority outside my home. I didn't hesitate at all. I had no fear. I jumped right in faith and backed the enemy off my property. How dare the enemy think he would mark up the property that God entrusted to me and gave to me?

To me it was like an instant reflex. I just knew I would win. When we revisit 1 Samuel 17:32 it says:

> *And David said to Saul, Let no man's heart fail because of him; thy servant will go and fight with this Philistine.*

It also appears that this was David's thought pattern. When you read the previous verses, David had inquired what would he get for defeating Goliath before he pledged going to battle. He desired to know what would be his reward. Once he found out he did not hesitate to act because David knew with God he would win!

Principle #7

<u>There is greater power in the prayer of agreement</u>. Matthew 18:19-20 say:

> *Again I say unto you, That if two of you shall agree on earth as touching any thing that they shall ask, it shall be done for them of my Father which is in heaven. 20. For where two or three are gathered together in my name, there am I in the midst of them.*

When you get a buy-in and participation from the people living in your house three things happen:

1. A higher – stronger power of agreement takes over the power of the enemy and your prayers accomplish their goals.
2. You operate in agreement and <u>shut all the doors to the enemy</u>.
3. Father God takes care of the matter personally for you.

Chapter 3:
Using the Jericho Principle

For as long as I can remember my Aunt Julia McPeace was in the tavern business. I called her "Ant Julia." The one place I vividly remember was a tavern on the corner of 69th and Carpenter, in Chicago, IL, called Julia's Lounge.

Ant Julia believed in selling liquor and keeping a place for people to drink and play cards. If she liked you, she was the nicest person to you. If she didn't, she could be the meanest person to get alone with.

One person she loved most beside her son and her men friends was her brother, my father, John D. Lee, Sr. I guess she considered my mom a threat to her relationship with my father because Ant Julia mostly gave my mother a hard time.

Ant Julia would do anything for my dad, even lie for him. So when my father won $10,000 on a lottery ticket, I'm glad my mother was there in the tavern that night. If Mama hadn't been there, she would have never found out about the money until it was completely spent or Daddy's friends had swindled it out of him through gambling.

Daddy quit his good paying job at the US Post Office driving a truck to open his dream restaurant across the street from his sister's tavern. Now the people could drink their drinks at his sister's tavern and go across the street to Lee's Fish Market for fresh fish and other short order food. Mama ran the fish market and built up the business so that we were finally making a profit when I was in high school.

Neither Daddy nor Ant Julia knew how to encourage people without putting them down. So one day Daddy struck out verbally at Dolores, my mama in the restaurant, and Mama quit. She went home. He said he could do the business by himself. Mama said "Fine, you do it then." But he couldn't he needed someone else's help.

Daddy hired a lady to do the job he had Mama doing. The new lady didn't work 14-16 hour days. Nor did this woman have the business sense my Mama had. Business went downhill from there.

Mama came back to the fish market about nine months later and there was very little business. She couldn't even build it back up. Eventually, they closed the "restaurant" as we called it. But Julia's Lounge was alive and kicking.

Fights continued to happen on the corner from people getting drunk. Families were torn up because of lies, betrayal, adultery, fornication, and alcoholism. Why Ant Julia herself had a couple of married boyfriends. Life in the tavern was full of destroying households and keeping people in bondage.

After the restaurant closed, Mama found herself a job at Goldblatt's at 3939 W. Madison on the Westside of Chicago, IL. Mama worked her way up from being a switchboard operator to the department manager of lingerie.

Daddy now worked with Ant Julia running her place. I went to college, got pregnant, married, had twin babies, and dropped out of college. We lived in my ex-mother-in-law's basement apartment, a block away from Julia's Lounge.

My Daddy died August 13, 1977 from an untreated ruptured appendicitis (they had diagnosed him with cancer) when my middle child was three months old. Mama and Ant Julia bonded for a while since they both were grieving my father's death.

When Goldblatt's went bankrupt about four years after my Daddy's death, Mama worked for Ant Julia because the Veterans Administration (VA) never gave her Daddy's pension.

Ant Julia started some of her old tricks. She demanded a lot from Mama as her sister-in-law. Yet, anything Mama got from Ant Julia she worked for. Mama worked her business sense and built up Julia's Lounge. But Ant Julia was jealous of Mama's success and did not treat Mama right. Eventually, Mama got fed up and left there again. Thus, Mama never had any control of Ant Julia's business.

Everyone called my Mama: "Mz. Lee or Mama." Mama had a warm heart and provided a listening ear. Most people considered her a second Mama or the mama they never had.

When my Mama left, change came to Julia's Lounge. Other taverns opened in the neighborhood. One of Ant Julia's married boyfriend's ran Julia's Lounge. People blatantly brought their marijuana into the tavern. Customers were getting younger and younger with different demands.

Actually the younger customers were the second generation of some of the older regular clients. All the regulars, the older clients, were: dying, staying at home, admitted into hospitals, or going elsewhere for their business (where the prices were cheaper). Taxes were on the rise. And the cost of licensing had increased.

Occasionally, my Ant Julia and Mama attended a church on Sunday that let out just in enough time for Ant Julia to open her tavern at 12 noon. Eventually, Mama went to a different church but Ant Julia stayed at the one close to 69th and Carpenter. She believed in participating in positive things when it didn't take her too far from the tavern.

By this time I had received Jesus Christ in my heart and was living a life for him. I took both Mama and Ant Julia to church with me one Sunday. A lady prophesied publicly over the congregation and Ant Julia vowed never to return to that church.

Some years later, I took an evangelist to Ant Julia's apartment over the tavern. I had been out previously with him and a team street witnessing. He wasn't afraid to enter the tavern with me to see her. He and I witnessed to Ant Julia and she received the Lord Jesus Christ in her heart. About a month later she died.

There was no money to bury her with. Ant Julia's current married-boyfriend and she spent it all. He also cashed-in the insurance policy early that would have buried her. We had no money either. The undertaker did something I never saw before. They buried her in a long cardboard box inside a metal container. Now, Ant Julia weighed over 300 lbs. It was a horrible sight: seeing her body oozing out of that box. There was no funeral or service. We just didn't have the money. We had just scraped up enough money for the burial plot.

Yet, people were still buying liquor at Julia's Lounge. Shortly after Ant Julia's death, Mama was summoned to court. Ant Julia's boyfriend was still running the tavern.

I never saw the summons so I can't say which agency it was whether it was the Licensing Commission, the State of Illinois, or Cook County. So I'll say the government demanded that Mama take care of all of Ant Julia's debts including her back taxes, fines, and unpaid licenses. And since the tavern was in such disrepair and literally falling apart, the government decided to tear down the tavern at Mama's expense.

Remember I said that Ant Julia could be nice or evil. Well, I meant it. The devil had been using Ant Julia to torment my Mama most of Mama's married life. I know a lot of it had to do with the fact that Mama was 18 years younger than Daddy and 20 years younger than Ant Julia.

So when Daddy was dying, Ant Julia showed up at the hospital while Mama was there with Daddy's current girlfriend, a woman he met at Julia's Lounge.

Moreover, when Daddy died, Ant Julia could have written a letter to the VA to let them know that Daddy's first daughter, Julia (her namesake), died when she was eight-years-old from a heart murmur and that Daddy's first wife divorced him.

The building holding all birth and death records in that town in Mississippi had been burned down. Julia's mama (the dead daughter's mother) claimed to be still married to Daddy, but Ant Julia wouldn't write the letter. Thus for 25 years until her death, Mama never received any of Daddy's VA money that she deserved as his legal wife.

Oh it gets better! Ant Julia also worried Mama about Daddy's social security number until Mama gave it to her. This was so the last baby boy born out of wedlock to that girlfriend could receive VA benefits: the same VA benefits that Mama never received.

So when the government talked about my Mama paying for Ant Julia's debts and the demolition of Julia's Lounge, a constant reminder of all the emotional pain Mama suffered. **I got angry with the devil**. I decided that the devil wasn't using Ant Julia to torment my Mama from the grave.

The tavern was still open by the same married boyfriend who ran it illegally **and the government never considered going after him to settle Ant Julia's debts**.

As I was reading in Joshua, I received revelation and decided that Julia's Lounge had to come down without Mama paying a single penny for it. In Joshua 6:1-21, God gave specific instructions about what to do for the walls of Jericho to come down. Jericho had these wide thick walls that were difficult to penetrate. These walls surrounded the city making it impossible for anyone to conquer the city.

Sort of like Ant Julia's mountain of debts the government desired my Mama to pay. She had no pension and a little disability check that had just started coming in. Mama had been laid off her job at Goldblatt's since they closed because of bankruptcy. Mama was worried.

I decided to take authority and I did not discuss it with Mama, I discussed it with God. I was tired of the lives and families in the neighborhood that had been destroyed by this place.

I asked God that Julia's Lounge come

down and Mama not have to pay a single penny for it. I had tried a smaller version of this revelation with my ex-husband. I'll share that situation now.

In 1983, I searched for my husband on Christmas Eve so that I could get the money I needed to buy Christmas gifts for our four daughters. (We were supposedly temporarily separated until he could get the gas turned back on at our house on 69th and Dorchester.)

I did not go alone. I took one of my brothers with me since it was late at night on Christmas Eve. I left our children with my other family members.

My brother stayed in the car and I banged on the apartment door. Someone told me my husband was there. A woman answered. This woman was larger than me in size and not as beautiful as I. She met my husband at Julia's Lounge.

I requested to speak with my husband. She went in and got him. The apartment was not that big. He staggered to the door. I asked where was the money for our children's Christmas gifts?

My husband had this glazed look on his face and shook his head to gather his wits. I guess he couldn't believe it was me, the mild manner Christian, demanding to know where was the money for our children's gifts and standing at his girlfriend's apartment.

This was a small basement studio apartment in the 69th block of Carpenter in Chicago, IL, next door to her mother's two-flat apartment building and around the block from his mother's two-flat apartment building. You could see from the doorway lots of Christmas gifts under the tree for someone!

I could not believe it! The man I loved and had had four children by was living and sleeping with someone else and not at his mother's house as he told me after he got off of work. Moreover, the children he supposedly loved were without Christmas gifts because he did something else with the money.

My husband slowly responded that he didn't have any money. Next, he wanted me to leave. He was defending his girlfriend (something he never did for me).

At that point, her sister materialized from the apartment building next door to tell me that I was destroying Christmas for them. My brother, who had been waiting in the car across the street walked up also.

I was furious. I looked at her and said,

"Christmas … Christmas! My children need Christmas too!!!"

The old me would have started a fight. The new me didn't. Instead I left. I desired to remain a Christian and not respond in anger to the mess. But I also desired that my children have something for Christmas.

I didn't even have enough food for them for that day. I do not remember how we made it through that Christmas but we did. I remember that was the Christmas we were staying with my relatives and they brought our daughters Christmas gifts.

I found out later that the reason why my husband didn't have any money was that he and his girlfriend spent the money on alcohol and drugs.

I gathered my wits, prayed, and consulted the Bible. I was angry and desired to do something in faith to maintain that I desired my husband and was not willing to let him go.

At first, I was angry with my husband, the woman, and the enemy. Then I got really angry with the situation. It did not have to come to that point. My husband could have just kept his promise to take care of our family and we could have moved on.

After reading the Bible and listening to Apostle JoAnn Long on the radio, I decided to do something spiritual. I drove in the day time to that apartment and stood on the steps. I pointed at the door and said out loud,

> "I bind every foul and unclean spirit. I take authority! From this point forward, there will be no peace in this place outside of the will of God in Jesus' name, amen."

I spoke in tongues and left.

I prayed all the way home and released everything to God. After that I put it out of my mind and did not go by that place for a while. I assessed my life and moved on. Some months later, my husband finally paid the gas bill and wanted us to come back home with him since he supposedly left his girlfriend.

In the process of trying to reconcile with him, I took the girls to see their paternal grandmother. Since it was right around the block from the studio basement apartment, I purposely drove down that block.

Startled by what I saw, I dropped the girls off and quickly came back around to see the results of my previous prayer up close. I got out of the car and walked up to the steps of that basement apartment.

The door had gang graffiti written all over it and it was boarded up. No one was living there. I smiled. It worked! God had come through for me!

After we moved back in together, my husband started leaving us alone again. It was close to winter and he had stopped paying the gas bill again. This time since that studio basement apartment was boarded up, I found out he was living next door to the studio apartment with his girlfriend in her mother's apartment building on the second floor.

I didn't hesitate. I drove up to that apartment, walked up those steps, and took authority again in the spirit realm. I released a similar prayer to the first one to God and I rested that God would do the rest. I did add one more item to the prayer that as long as he was there and not with his own family; there would be no peace.

Some months later, I drove by the apartment again taking the girls to see their grandmother. This time the second apartment building also was boarded up with huge weeds in front of it. My prayers had worked again! I heard later that the girlfriend's family moved on 67th street between Racine and May streets.

Since I had results before after reading in Joshua about Jericho, I believed that God was letting me know to use the Jericho principle on Mama's situation. Moreover this time, I was not going to be afraid and partially work the principle. I made up my mind to completely work the Jericho Principle.

Listening carefully to the spirit of God, I acted right away. By this time Mama watched my children after work and I paid her. So I told her that I would be a little late picking them up that week. For the strategy to work I had to be consistent at the same time for the next seven consecutive days.

Each day for five days I went straight to Julia's Lounge after work. On the weekend I got Mama to watch the children while I went to Julia's Lounge in the afternoon.

On the week days, I arrived around 5:45 pm or 6 pm due to traffic. I got out of the car and walked silently around the building. I did not speak to anyone, which was totally unusual for me because Mama taught me to speak to everyone. According to Mama, it was rude not to speak to people when I encountered them.

That was not the hard part. The hard part was walking through the vacate lot adjacent to the tavern. The weeds were tall and there were huge rats going in and out of the basement of Julia's Lounge that I was truly afraid of. I went in faith and thank God I did not see one rat. The angels knew what to do.

Next was dealing with the people. By the third day this man stood on the step of Julia's Lounge watching me walk around the building. On the fourth day that man tried to talk to me when I walked in silence. I did not respond.

On the fifth day as I finished walking around in silence and got into my car, he came out of Julia's Lounge and ran up to a woman walking by and asked her if I had just walked around the building.

When the seventh day came, I walked around the building six times in silence. That same man wasn't standing on the step of the tavern watching. However by the seventh time around as I finished shouting and completing my final walk around the building, he came running out of the tavern, got directly in my face, and shouted at me. I still didn't say a word.

I got in my car, praised God all the way to Mama's house for the victory; and picked up my children. I was truly thankful for completing my assignment and expected to see the results.

About four months later, Mama went to

court again. This time the government decided that Mama didn't have to pay for Ant Julia's debts. Nor did Mama have to pay for the demolition of Julia's Lounge. Mama was very relieved and happy. She slept through the entire night for the first time in a long time.

As of today, March 19, 2010, there is a vacant leveled spot on the northwest corner of 69th and Carpenter where Julia's Lounge used to be (1034 West 69th Street, Chicago, IL 60621). Praise God! And my Mama, Dolores A. Davis Lee didn't have to pay for it. She did not pay a penny! It is no longer a place where neighborhood families are destroyed. Hallelujah!

Principle #8

<u>Only God can fix it</u>. I didn't have any extra money. As a matter of fact, I did not desire to help Mama pay for Ant Julia's tavern. I didn't agree with paying for it. My desire was to get rid of it a long time ago when it was causing my Mama emotional pain with my Daddy and for me with my husband.

The amount of money required to handle this was too much for me. I did not have any answers. I could only take it to God, my Daddy-Father God, who has all the answers!

I found out that what is impossible with

man is possible with God (Matthew 19:26b). It was impossible for Mama to get rid of Ant Julia's debts with her little disability money but in one day, God got rid of it!

Principle #9

Revelation from God gives you courage to do what He instructs. I did not know what to do but I knew I had the power to do something. I prayed and read my bible to discover what I was to do and I did it. And I was not afraid to do it. I had no fear!

I would have never thought that using the Jericho Principle would end my Mama's debts without that revelation from God.

Principle #10

Once you take action, leave it in God's hands. At first in the natural, Julia's Lounge was still up. But in the spirit realm when I finished my last walk around and shouted, Julia's Lounge came down. **It was a done deal to me! The angels and God went to work!** I did not wait until I heard from Mama thinking: did God come through or will it ever happen? **I knew God did!**

After that I waited for the physical manifestation in faith, joy, and peace. I rested. And I never told anybody even Mama until now what God and I did.

Chapter 4:
Changing my Neighborhood

In 1988, when my twin daughters were 13-years-old, we lived at 10449 South Racine, in Chicago, IL. Next door lived this woman, her children, and her brothers in the corner house. She had taken over the house after her mother died and as the oldest sister, she raised her younger brothers and two sons together.

One of the older brothers was the neighborhood drug dealer. When I moved in the neighborhood, there was little noticeable activity by him.

However, the illegal business increased in spring and by the summer; the drug dealer, his brothers, and their friends began having other activities at night. The outdoor party started around 9 p.m.

They drank hard liquor and beer. They shot craps on the corner of 105th and Racine near the curb. They played cards, loud music, and sold drugs to those passing by until about 4 a.m. With no school, their children played outside during these times until the adults went to bed. It was difficult for anyone who had a legal job to sleep at night.

We had no air conditioning and the only air that circulated through the second floor was from the open windows. It was too hot to keep them close. While my children could sleep through anything, I could not sleep through that music and noise.

After about four consecutive nights of this during the week, I decided I had enough. I drove over an hour each morning to get to work and I didn't know about my neighbors but I had to do something to stop this madness. Besides because of the lack of sleep at night, I had begun pulling up to the toll booths and falling asleep behind the wheel. It had become dangerous for me.

Since I had started walking to improve my health, I decided to prayer walk through out the neighborhood. I initially just prayed as I walked around the blocks.

Once I got a little rest, I decided to walk right through the middle of their party territory. This meant that whether I got up to go to work during the week or on Saturdays, I prayed in the spirit in tongues against the success of their nightly activities.

The last straw was when I witnessed the drug dealer's 10-year-old son exchanging drugs for cash to one of his father's friends or clients on the side of their car in the middle of the street. It was one thing for the father to sell drugs. But for him to have his son selling drugs that was another issue. I got angry with the enemy and changed the way I prayed.

I pondered about all the people living in that one house. I also reviewed the negative influence the father was to his son. I asked my prayer partner at that time to pray with me. We prayed for wisdom and asked God to put the enemy off that corner and prayed something like the following:

> "Father in the name of Jesus, we thank you that you care about this family. We realize they are business people. We ask that you give every man in that house a legal job. Let them stop selling drugs. We bind them from being successful drinking, gambling, and partying on the street.
>
> Anyone who doesn't want to get a legal job then let them go to jail, in Jesus name, amen."

Next, I personally walked through their party territory and prayed the same thing right on the spot while the party bunch was still in bed recovering from the previous night's activities.

I found out that the prayer of agreement

and prayer on the spot are powerful. It didn't happen right away. But God answered our prayers. I continued walking through the party territory and I even pointed directly at the house and spoke that every male would get a legitimate job or go to jail. I also continued to pray in the spirit as I walked.

Slowly but surely one by one each male in the house found a legitimate job except the drug dealer. With legitimate jobs that started early in the morning, the party changed. There was no brother to party with and make sure the money was right; so the nightly activities ceased.

Since the drug dealer didn't desire a legitimate job or look for one, he was carted off to jail. His 10-year-old son was sent to Milwaukee, WI to live with his mother.

The people, who used to just drive up quickly in their cars any time of day, had to find another drug source. Parents relaxed that their children could play on the block without worrying about them being involved in a drug deal gone bad.

That neighborhood became quiet again. People slept at night in the summer with the gentle night breeze flowing through their open windows in peace: God's peace.

With legitimate jobs, the other brothers moved out of that house one by one into their own places. These brothers grew up into mature responsible adults. And eventually that woman raised only her two boys in that huge house.

As long as I lived in that neighborhood at 10449 South Racine, Chicago, IL, the nightly activities never revived. We all enjoyed a peaceful rest at night.

Principle #11

Recognize and use the weapons God has given you. It is important to use the right weapon in your situation. When I discussed my situation with my prayer partner; we used God's weapon of the prayer of agreement to combat the situation. We based it on Matthew 18:19 (AMP), which says:

> *Again I tell you, if two of you on earth agree (harmonize together, make a symphony together) about whatever [anything and everything] they may ask, it will come to pass and be done for them by My Father in heaven.*

We had to recognize that this applied to this situation and realize it was up to us to use this weapon against the enemy.

Principle #12

Put your faith in action. Faith requires that you do something to activate it. James 2:17 (KJV) says,

> Even so faith, if it hath not works, is dead, being alone.

Throughout the bible once God gave a directive or revelation then He required the person participating in faith to do some type action for God's results to manifest. So I put my faith in action when I walked through the sidewalk/curbside party area.

Principle #13

Take the territory back! I claimed territory just like in Joshua 1:3 (KJV) which says,

> Every place that the sole of your foot shall tread upon, that have I given unto you, as I said unto Moses.

The enemy had invaded our neighborhood. It was time to recover our peaceful neighborhood and evict the enemy out of our territory. Moreover, we didn't have to ask the enemy for his permission to evict him. We asked God.

In September 2009, I moved into a different

apartment building. It is a two-story building with 28 apartments in Oak Lawn, IL. After about a month, I started watching one of the other tenants. At first, I was not sure but it appeared as if he was selling drugs.

He was friendlier than usual even though he was in a relationship. There was always a party going on at his place. (I have nothing against an occasional party.) But constantly a lot of different types of people entered in and out of the apartment he shared with his girlfriend across the hallway from my apartment.

Next, this man stood on the door step of the building often late at night right outside of my window. He waited for someone to drive up to the entrance of the building then he pass something to the driver or someone sitting in the car. It didn't just happen once but a couple of times. Next, one of the tenants openly accused him of doing drugs.

Once I realized I was right about what was going on; I refuse to put up with that type of activity in the building that I live in … **in my neighborhood**. I didn't call the police. I went to my higher power. I simply asked God in prayer for him to be removed.

Not too long after the prayer early the Saturday morning after Thanksgiving in 2009, his girlfriend evicted him from their apartment with the assistance of the Oak Lawn Police Department. He had just started a new legal job. He kept calling her name and saying,

> "(........), don't do this to me! I just started working my job. Just let me shower so I can go to work."

They had been partying all night and the neighbors next door to me had gotten into a fight because of the party. No, the police did not take him away to jail for drugs. They just escorted him out of the building, off the property, and out of our neighborhood. He was totally evicted!

My prayer had been answered and I was satisfied. He tried a couple of times since then to come back into the building but it did not happen. Honestly, I didn't care who God used as long as the drug activity was gone.

Principle #14

It is up to me to exercise my authority. God gave me dominion (Genesis 1:28) in the Old Testament. In the New Testament, Jesus explained how much power I have as a Christian. It says in Luke 10:19 (AMP):

> *Behold! I have given you authority and power to trample upon serpents*

and scorpions, and [physical and mental strength and ability] over all the power that the enemy [possesses]: and nothing shall in any way harm you.

It is up to me to use my power. God expects me to take dominion. If I never take the lead and take authority over my neighborhood, I leave the neighborhood in the hands and at the mercy of the enemy. That same enemy gives no mercy and only takes.

If I as a Christian have the authority to change my neighborhood and you are a Christian then **you have that same authority**. We serve a loving Father who is not a respecter of persons. God is waiting on you to step up and change your neighborhood.

You do not have to put up with drug dealers or gang bangers in your neighborhood or your own household. **You can pray**. You do not have to pray in their faces or where they can see you. You not have to pray for their demise because some Christians used to be gang bangers, gang members, and drug dealers. **You can pray for them to get legitimate jobs and receive the Lord Jesus Christ in their hearts**.

I have shown you ways God had me to do it. Now it is up to you! Through prayer and in faith **you have the power** to take dominion and authority. Can God count on you to be the person in this earth who spiritually cleans up a neighborhood? Will you change your neighborhood, bring it peace, establish safety for your neighbors, and **take territory back for God**?

Chapter 5:
Receiving Jesus Christ
in Your Heart

All the information in this book is effective if you have received Jesus Christ in your heart and you live for him. If you have not done this then it is very easy to do. I received Jesus Christ in my heart over the telephone at work during my 15-minute morning break.

Romans 3:23 (KJV) says,

> "*For all have sinned, and come short of the glory of God;*"

Scriptures Romans 10:9-10 (KJV) say,

> "*That if thou shalt confess with thy mouth the Lord Jesus, and shalt believe in thine heart that God hath raised him from the dead, thou shalt be saved. For with the heart man believeth unto righteousness and with the mouth confession is made unto salvation.*"

Romans 10:13 (KJV) says,

> "*For whosoever shall call upon the name of the Lord shall be saved.*"

To receive the Lord Jesus Christ in your heart, say these next words out loud.

Father in the name of Jesus, I repent of my sins. I ask you to forgive me of my sins. I ask you to come into my heart and be my Lord and be my savior. I believe that Jesus Christ was God in the flesh and died on the cross for my sins.

Jesus, live your life in me and through me from this time forward. Right now I am saved. Thank you for saving me, in Jesus' name, Amen.

If you said that prayer out loud, know that you are saved right now! Welcome to the family of the Lord Jesus Christ. Hallelujah!

If you need to rededicate your life to Jesus again because you are living like you were never saved, smoking dope, drinking every day, and/or beating your wife/husband, then you can rededicate your life to Jesus now. **Say the same previous prayer**.

Once you have said that prayer, understand there is now no condemnation, which includes no guilt. Romans 8:1 (KJV) says,

There is therefore no condemnation to

> *them which are in Christ Jesus, who walk not after the flesh, but after the Spirit.*

Second Corinthians 5:17 (KJV) says,

> *Therefore if any man be in Christ, he is a new creature: old things are passed away; behold all things are become new.*

Psalm 103:12 (KJV) says,

> *As far as the east is from the west, so far hath he removed our transgressions from us.*

Our transgressions are our sins. God wipes the slate clean on our history and our life of sin.

First John 1:9 (KJV) says,

> *If we confess our sins, he is faithful and just to forgive us our sins, and to cleanse us from all unrighteousness.*

If God can forgive us, release us, and wipe the slate clean, then we can forgive ourselves and walk in a new life. Our life in Jesus is our new life, Hallelujah!

If you would like to receive the baptism of

Holy Spirit? You can today. (Holy Spirit and Holy Ghost are synonymous titles.) Holy Spirit is a free gift from God. Acts 1:8 (KJV) says,

> *But ye shall receive power, after that the Holy Ghost is come upon you: and ye shall be witnesses unto me both in Jerusalem, and in Judea, and in Samaria, and unto the uttermost part of the earth.*

Holy Spirit gives you additional dynamic power to resist the enemy (the devil—satan). Understand that this means that Holy Spirit will live inside of you just like the Lord Jesus. Holy Spirit will speak to you and guide you into all truth. To receive Holy Spirit, please say the next prayer.

> *Father in the name of Jesus, I thank you I am born again. I am your child, Hallelujah! You said in Luke 11:13 (KJV) "If ye then, being evil, know how to give good gifts unto your children: how much more shall your heavenly Father give the Holy Spirit to them that ask him?"*
>
> *So right now, I ask You to fill me with Holy Spirit. I rise up and praise you God for your free gift. I expect to speak with other tongues as You*

*give me utterance as according to
Acts 2:4 in Jesus' name, Amen.*

If you said either prayer and received
Jesus Christ in your heart or the baptism of
Holy Spirit, please write us and let us know.
We can be reached at:

God's Heartbeat LLC
P. R. Lee
9624 South Cicero #414
Oak Lawn, IL, 60453.

You may contact us by email at:

admin@godsheartbeat-inc.com
Or at:
godsheartbeat_inc@yahoo.com